Sweatpants & Stilettos

RACHEL N. CLEVELAND

Copyright © 2015 Rachel N. Cleveland

All rights reserved.

ISBN-13: 978-0-692-43508-3

Published in the United States by Xilo Media

Lewisville, TX

For Felicity, Heidi, Caroline and Rose.

May you all grow to be gracious women of God

and courageous beacons of His light

CONTENTS

Acknowledgments

1	Before	11
2	Starting Out	13
3	The Breakdown	21
4	The Darkness	27
5	Memorials	33
6	The Cycle	45
7	Endurance	51
8	Lost	55
9	Idols	59
10	Choosing Joy	69
11	Love	75
12	Peace	83
13	Marriage	87
14	Waiting	95
15	Outlets	101
16	Losing It	107
17	Art of Busyness	119
18	That One Thing	133
19	Begin Again	141
	Closing	149
	Sights and Sounds	153

ACKNOWLEDGMENTS

This would not have been possible without so many people who encouraged me, laughed with me, cried with me, and told me I had something worth telling.

To my family who loves me no matter what- thank you for always allowing me to follow my gut.

To Matthew for letting me force my way into your life and tolerating my tears.

To Liz, Ann, Brittany, Jenny, Kristin, and McCauley who would spend hours on the phone with me, no matter how far away I was, and keep me sane, smiling through tears, and moving forward.

To Billy, the captain and best boss in the world, for listening, praying, and mentoring me through some very dark days.

And finally, to my students who inspire me everyday with their genuine passion for life and their quick-wittedness.

I will look up for there is none above you
I will bow down to tell you that I need you
Jesus, Lord of all
Jesus, Lord of all

I will look back and see that you are faithful
I look ahead believing you are able
Jesus, Lord of all
Jesus, Lord of all

-Elevation Worship

1
BEFORE

So I read a book that challenged me to do something I've always wanted to do. A hidden talent that has been buried for years, but should be dug up. My dear friend and sorority little, Jessica, sent me the Annie Downs' book "Let's All Be Brave" was a call to arms really; a call to live a courageous life through small steps every day. One of those hidden talents for me is writing. I love it. I've kept journals since I was in kindergarten (not kidding, I still have the journals). Mostly I wrote about liking my teachers or some boy in my class. But still I was writing.

I love to write thank you notes for anything. The practice of using pen and paper and putting a stamp on it (does anyone else still do this?) makes me happy. I write notes to my kids (I don't actually have kids of my own, but I'll explain that later), Christmas cards to friends, lists of things to do (oh, how I love to write to-do lists!!), anything really. Because sometimes, the old fashioned way is the best. And seeing as I'm coming out of the most difficult year of my young life, writing seemed like a good way to wrap this all up and start the New Year off well. So I guess I'll give it a try.

Note to reader, I am no professional. You will need to bear with me as I do my best to convey the deep pain and luminous glory I have experienced this year. I pray God's love will encourage your heart as you read my story.

2
STARTING OUT

To start, I figure you should know a few things about me. First, I am that girl that has been to church just about every Sunday of my life. I grew up attending with my family and was baptized at a young age. I don't remember the whole process, or the decision like some people do. I do, however, remember feeling clean. Feeling new. Feeling valued. From then on I was at everything the church offered me for my age group, up through college.

I attended great churches at home and at school and was involved in all of them. When I returned to Texas from

Nashville (I went to the most amazing school in Nashville-Belmont University. Go Bruins!), I began to work with the children's choir at my church, was part of the singles ministry, and then eventually start teaching 5th and 6th grade girls Sunday school classes. I was a church guru you might say. I loved Jesus (still do) and enjoyed being part of the different ministries that taught His truths.

Second, I have the best job in the world. Seriously. I say it all the time. Because it is true. I'm on staff at the University of North Texas in the College of Business. I am the assistant director of a program that develops students for their careers after college through mentoring and soft skills development, all with a servant leadership mentality. I really love what I do.

These students are my kids. Every day is different and challenging. I was made to do this job (for now) and I have been incredibly blessed to work with some of the most amazing people in the world. I don't say that to make it sound perfect, but honestly, they are the best and our students are phenomenal.

Third, I'm kind of a fashion person. What I mean by that is, I like to find great clothes that I feel great in. What I do not mean is that I wear the highest fashions and go out to spend thousands of dollars on the latest trend. Don't get me wrong, I like to tastefully put together outfits that make me feel confident and collected. I own leather pants and a leather skirt which I wear in a professional setting (and pull off if I do say so myself). I own a couple of great pairs of shoes, statement necklaces, adorable winter jackets, and enjoy Fossil bags. I say all this to say I like fashion but it is not my calling in life like it can be for some people.

Something I have learned about fashion is that it either has to match your mood or improve it. So many months of this year were what I call the sweatpants days. Don't even try to tell me you don't understand what I mean by that statement. But just so we are all on the same page, sweatpants days are those days that all you want to do is stay in bed with your sweatpants on and have Netflix at your beck and call. They are the days in which the sun should not shine, the world should not move on, and no one should smile, laugh or be happy.

Thankfully, I have also learned this year that sweatpants days don't last forever. I have seen them go from sweatpants to jean days to leather pant days and then on to stiletto days. Those are the days where you feel the absolute best and are 100% yourself, doing what you were created to do, with people you love to be around, and everything is falling into place. Blessings from heaven abound. Yeah. Those days. They are the stiletto days. They are the take-on-the-world, tell-them-who's-boss, no-one-can-stop-you kind of days. And they are awesome. I love those days.

This year started out with stiletto days non-stop. I was starting my second year at UNT (the best job in the entire world... Have I told you that enough yet?), I had amazing friends, family was all doing well, the nieces were growing in leaps and bounds, the Lord was providing, volunteering at church was great, everything at work was flowing, hard work was paying off, and I was enjoying every day with a smile. Literally every day. You can ask my friends, they all found it super annoying because I was so happy.

In our office, my boss called it "The Cleveland Effect." Everything I seemed to touch or be involved with did well and flourished. I laughed when he dubbed the new phrase, but then I started to see it too, and finally came around to believing the Lord was blessing me tremendously. "The Cleveland Effect" was in full swing. That was the spring semester. (Since I work in education, my life runs in semesters.) We graduated the largest class ever from our program in its 20 year history, after celebrating the anniversary in a grand gala. (Goodness, if you could have seen me planning a gala… beautiful chaos). And we recruited an even larger class to begin participation in the fall semester for the year-long program.

Work wasn't the only thing going great. Personally, I spent the first half of the year working my butt off and lost 40 pounds. Yeah, I was looking great and feeling even better! I had been accepted into the doctoral program to pursue my doctorate of education in higher education (I'm a nerd, can't help it). I had finally found a new place to move closer to school and work, cutting my (time) commute down to (new time). And I was about to head to London and Scotland for a 15-day, well-earned, vacation. I know you are thinking 'what 27-year-old does that?'. But traveling is a huge passion of mine. It's one of those things that I will spend money on. Shoes, meh. Technology, eh. Plane tickets and tours, sign me up! So basically, I was about to embark on a whole new chapter of life and things couldn't be better or look brighter.

The trip started well. I was spending 6 days in London then another 6 days in Edinburgh with my parents and some family friends that are basically my second parents and their daughter. We were all traveling to see my sister perform in Edinburgh with the New Life Symphony Orchestra.

Another thing you should know about me: I come from a musical family. We all had to take piano lessons growing up. My dad and I both sing. My sister plays oboe. My brother played in the marching band in high school. My mom plays piano, flute, and sings. And my oldest brother sings too, but played more baseball than music growing up. We aren't famous or wildly talented, but we enjoy it and offer our talents as often as we can.

So back to the trip. It was the third day into the London stint. We had seen the Queen's jubilee festivities for her birthday (I saw Kate Middleton!!), did the whole platform 9 ¾ thing at King's Cross, shopping at Harrods, took high tea every chance I could, and had gone to a musical on Drury Lane. Picturesque experience, really. Then I got the call.

3
THE BREAKDOWN

It was one of those middle-of-the-night, never-could-imagine, this-can't-possibly-be-true calls. I was in a time zone six hours ahead of home, so it was around 3 am when the calls started to come in. Two of my students were trying to reach me around the same time. I was out of the country and didn't have international calls. So I iMessaged them on the hotel WIFI asking what was up, reminding them I was in London and asking if it could wait until I got home. You know, the normal response to being woken up in the middle of the night. On vacation. By your kids. In response, I got screenshots of a story outlining an accident that occurred in

Houston, Texas, in the wee hours of Father's Day. Something had happened.

I slowly began to read the articles thinking my students had lost someone and were looking for comforting words of encouragement. Told you, they are my kids. We are that close. Then I got to the point where the news article explained how a drunk driver had caused an accident involving five cars and one young female had not survived the crash. The next screenshot was of a memorial post already on Facebook regarding my dear student, Alexia Ardeleanu. Then I realized, it wasn't just my students who had lost someone, I had too.

Alexia had served as president of our program that year. She had spent countless hours in my office working on meeting agendas, training ideas, asking questions about life, and venting on the stress of being a double major

(Accounting and Finance), Resident Assistant, Honor's College student, and working a 30-hour internship. She was a 4.0 stellar student. A caring woman of incredible patience and willingness to serve in any way she could.

I couldn't believe she was gone. It wasn't possible. She was the best of the best, had the brightest future and was going to change the world. She had just turned 21 a few months ago. She couldn't be dead. But she was and I wept. And not the pretty kind of tears. No, it was the gut-wrenching, uncontrollable, can't breathe kind of crying. For hours. There are tears slipping down my face now as I type this and it has been 6 months since her accident.

The next day we toured Westminster Abbey. I had seen it before (I told you I like to travel), but went into the gift shop to warm up. For a day in June, London had turned into a cold, drizzly day, which was fine with me as it fit my mood perfectly. In the gift shop I wandered, unseeing for awhile until my eyes finally focused on a necklace. Now, I'm not Catholic, nor do I believe in praying to saints, but I found a charm with Saint Christopher on it, the patron saint of travel. He is pictured carrying baby Jesus across a raging river. I felt it was appropriate, as Alexia had passed away while traveling, to serve as a memorial token. To this day, I wear the necklace often to honor her memory.

I spent the next few days crying without even noticing. I would be fine one minute, distracted by the beautiful landscape of England and Scotland, and then all of the sudden burst into tears. One day we were at the Victoria and Albert Museum and there was a display of wedding dresses through the decades. It was beautiful and fun to walk through, and then somewhere between the 1970s display and the 1980s, I realized Alexia would never get the chance to wear a wedding dress. She would never have the joy of choosing her perfect gown or planning the one day almost every girl looks forward to. I lost it, to say the least.

Do you know how weird it feels to walk out of a wedding exhibit in tears? Those poor museum people probably thought I was crazy. I'm sure they were creating stories where I called off a wedding or was left at the altar or something. Who knows. I didn't care at the time. Now I'm sure I looked like a crazy, distressed, former bride. I sat in the lobby until my breathing became normal again. I wasn't watching the clock, but it felt like hours I spent on that bench. I'm sure it was only 15 minutes. That was the first day I was truly thankful for waterproof mascara.

After that day, I questioned if I should go home early from the trip to be with my students. At least if I was stateside I could help carry the load of questions, coordinate emails or visitations, or anything really. I felt like I should be there, but I wasn't. The guilt was overwhelming but the need for me to stay with my family was what I knew I had to do. I had many people encourage me to stay. My close friends, even my boss, told me to stay and he was dealing with this loss as much as I was in addition to managing the calls, emails, and speaking with her family. There was nothing for me to do back at home that would help anyone more than letting myself grieve.

Except I had no idea how to grieve. The only people I had lost in my life up to that point were my grandparents. And they were elderly and sick. It felt different than this sudden loss. This was something entirely strange to me. And powerful. It started with tears, grew into guilt, led me to doubt, and left me in despair.

4
THE DARKNESS

For anyone who has lost someone close to them, either unexpectedly or with some warning, you know it is never easy. For that person to be so young, makes it even more difficult, I think. After losing Alexia, my world was filled with tears and sorrow. I cried more than I thought possible. I spent many nights curled up in bed praying the Lord would just take the pain away so I could sleep. Except when I slept, I had dreams. Dreams of normal days at the office and she would be there to help with some project. Dreams of other friends dying in accidents and me watching from a distance, unable to help. I'd wake up screaming and crying even more. Many mornings that meant I was at the gym at 3 AM working out until I was able to sweat more than I had just cried. Then I'd shower, cover up the dark circles, go to work, and try to act as normal as possible. Compensating sleep deprivation with extra cups of coffee and tea ended up making me sick. Literally ill. That part's a long story.

I tried to keep life as steady as possible. I continued reading my Bible, writing in my journal, going through the motions of life in order to maintain some normalcy. I was honest with the Lord about my pain, but not really anyone else. I spoke to others briefly about the hurt, but not the side effects. Mostly because every time I tried to speak, I'd just end up in tears. And I was tired of crying. So very tired of crying.

In the middle of the first few months that followed the tragedy, this verse was in my morning reading. "So the Lord must wait for you to come to him, so he can show you his love and compassion. For the Lord is a faithful God. Blessed are those who wait for his help." (Isaiah 30:18 NLT). In the midst of all my darkness, I was given this? At first I was angry. Why in the world would the Lord give this verse? How many times had He waited on me to come to him? Thousands? Was He waiting now? Why was I so easily distracted? Is this what it had taken to get my attention? Was being broken or lost the only way for me to fully see His love for me?

Now you older and wiser Christians are sitting there saying, "Well yes, Rachel that is often how the Lord works." Ok dear brothers and sisters, this was my first time to see it at this depth and man did it suck. I'm sure that's not the best word to use here, but it's my book. And it was awful. Painful. I was broken and lost, left alone, and lacking direction and motivation, two things I usually never need. Again, ask my friends and they will tell you. Why did the Lord take me from everything I knew, move me to a town that didn't fit my personality, and then dump the biggest bombshell of my life on me ALL AT THE SAME TIME? WHY? What was the point?

A few days later, I found another verse in Isaiah. "When you go through deep waters, I will be with you. When you go through rivers of difficulty, you will not drown… because you are precious to me. You are honored, and I love you" (Isaiah 43: 2a & 4b NLT). So at this point, I'm sitting there thinking: First, You tell me You are waiting on me to come to You so You can show me Your love. Now You are saying that on the journey through deep waters You will be with me? Am I getting that right, Lord?

You are with me and I am precious? I'm honored and You really do love me?

I've read the Word my whole life it seems. I've taught it. I've memorized it. I have it posted on my office walls, painted it in my apartment décor, and allowed it to rule my life. But right now, in all of this, He wanted me to know He was with me. Even when I didn't feel like it, or entirely want to believe it, because who lets their "honored" or "precious" one feel like this? Who does that? A loving Father does. In order to discipline His child, to keep them on the right path, to build character, to develop strength, to ready them for the fight, to show His glory and power. That is what a Father does for a loved child.

5
MEMORIALS

I have had the honor of speaking at two funerals in the past 12 months. By honor I mean that I was asked to remember people I love dearly and miss terribly. But honored or not, it was most likely two of the most difficult speeches I have ever written and then had to deliver.

I want to share these two memorials with you for two reasons. One, so that you will have a glimpse into two beautiful women who have help shaped my life over the years. And two, that you will see the impact remembering has on the lives of those of us still here on this earth.

Remembering their legacy is not for their benefit, it is for ours and it is for the benefit of others that we tell their story to the best of our ability.

Grandma

Our Grandma was many things to me. Growing up she was my babysitter and daycare teacher. She would watch Erin (my sister) and I while Mom was at Bible study or running errands. She played with us, or let us play while she watched soap operas on TV. She would make us lunch where we sat at the kids' table just our size in their kitchen; us eating peanut butter sandwiches with tiny boxes of raisins and her enjoying her onion sandwich. I have yet to understand the appeal of her choice in sandwiches! She made us nap, or tried to make us nap. I know for a fact I was the worst at this, probably adding to her grey hair every time she tried to convince me sleep was a good thing.

She always started by singing the Quakers' meeting song, which goes like this: "Quakers' meeting has begun. No more laughing, no more fun. If you dare to crack a smile, you will have to walk a mile." Now she never made me walk a mile, but that doesn't mean I followed the rules either.

Besides being our babysitter, she was the family historian. She had stories that could go on for days about everyone in our family, living or not. And she would tell you every single one of them if you gave her the time or, you know, sat too long in one place.

She also served as a role model to me in many ways. She loved our family and Grandpa faithfully all her life. She supported us in whatever we did and made sure we knew she loved us even from miles away. I remember when our family moved to Texas (before email was a thing) and she wrote us long, handwritten letters all the time. Birthdays, Easter, Christmas, any excuse to send a card and a long letter inside. We knew she and Grandpa loved us, even if it took us hours to figure out her insane handwriting. And it wasn't just us, she sent letters to everyone. Sharing stories and encouragement through her pen.

Probably the most important thing Grandma passed on to us was her faith. She loved her Savior passionately and unashamedly. And she shared that with everyone. People she knew, people she didn't, nurses who came to the house, anyone and everyone. She wanted all to know Christ and know His love for them. She always wanted that for our family. In fact, I don't remember a time when we were together in which Jesus wasn't mentioned, a prayer wasn't lifted or a hymn wasn't sung. Her love for Christ infiltrated her whole life and shone brightly to all the world around her.

She also served as a role model of a classy lady. She never left the house without her shoes matching her handbag, had a different set of earrings for every outfit, and never went anywhere without her lipstick on. In fact, one time we were leaving church to head home for the evening and I remember Grandpa gently saying, "Hurry up Ruthie." When I asked what she was doing, she told me she was putting her lipstick on. I laughed and said "Grandma, we are just going home. No one is going to see you." She ignored me and said, "Doesn't matter. There's nothing wrong with being prepared and looking your best." She was the fashion guru.

So today, I took her advice. I've worn my lipstick and brought this tube for her. I know today in heaven she is singing with the angels and Grandpa, and standing in the presence of her King. I know she is prepared and looking her best, but a little extra lipstick can't hurt.

Alexia Ardeleanu

Alexia has made a lasting impression on my life, just as she touched the lives of all who knew her. This evening you will hear just a few of the countless stories of praise and gratitude for the life she lived. In the past few weeks, I have been fortunate to hear and read many of these accounts and I am honored to add my own tonight.

Alexia was a brilliant young lady with an extraordinary heart to serve others. In fact, I often had to remind her of the importance of taking care of herself, in addition to everyone else, so she wouldn't burn out. She would spend countless hours in my office asking questions, seeking guidance, and talking about her goals. Despite her initial intention of seeking my help, she never left without checking to see what I needed or if there was something that she could help with. She always maintained a focus on others and never hesitated to address a need, big or small in scope.

A while back I came across some writings of a favorite author of mine, Jon Acuff, these words so inspired me that I kept them written down for a very long time. I knew if I were at the end of my life I would want someone to be able to say this of me. Here are a portion of his reflections.

"If at the end of my life, the only thing I've fought for is my own name, my days have been wasted.
If at the end of my life, the only thing I've cared about is my own care, my days have been wasted.

If at the end of my life, the only thing I've traded are works for rewards, my days have been wasted.

May we not go to the grave quietly.

May we not make refuse of the gifts we've been given.

May we never chase the shiny in place of the holy, the trend instead of the truth, the immediate instead of the eternal.

Arrive empty to the grace, having given all you were given, stewarded all you were tasked with.

Give the grave only bones."

This was our Alexia. She fought for the name of others, cared for the well-being of all who were around her, and did so without ever asking for anything in return. I know with great certainty that she was welcomed into heaven having given all she could to those in her life. She arrived to the grave with only bones to give. She never left anything undone or unresolved, but gave all she had to every task in front of her. And that memory of her is what will stay with us. Her legacy of a servant's heart, a hard work ethic, and exceptional stewardship of all she was given, is what we will hang on to for the months and years to come. For those reasons and countless others, she will never be forgotten.

To this day, this poem continues to challenge me. It makes me stop and think: what am I doing? It is impactful? Am I giving the grave only bones today? Only bones. Just those words give me chills as I sit and type. Is what I'm doing today, this very instant, changing the world around me in a positive or negative way? Am I doing the best with the resources, talents, and tools I have been given? Give the grave only bones.

I challenge you to take a moment to reflect on these words for yourself. What does giving the grave only bones look like for you? How would it change your life if you lived in such a way that at the end of your days, you only had bones to give this world and a crown of glory for the Heavenly One?

Since the memorial where I shared this poem with students, friends, and Alexia's family, they have remained at the forefront of my mind and my office. Many months later, her parents presented my boss and me with a memorial gift of Alexia. In this beautiful frame alongside a photograph of young, stunning Alexia, are written the words of this poem. It sits on my desk, in my office, as a reminder to treat today with the passion and tenacity befitting of Alexia and to leave nothing left to give.

On a side note, a memorial scholarship was created in Alexia's honor for students who have shown the same servant leadership Alexia exuded everyday. You can donate online at the link that follows. All funds are awarded to University of North Texas students who are also members of the Professional Leadership Program. May we all strive to live a life that leaves only bones left behind in the dirt and a legacy of grace and love to those whom we hold so dear.

Donate at one.unt.edu/alexia

6
THE CYCLE

With suffering, there are good days and bad ones. Many days this past fall would occur unmarked by memories, many others did not. I had days of real happiness and several with deep sorrow. I cried in front of people I would never have dreamed of crying in front of. Mostly because the pain was too much to put into words and my world was closing in on me. Or so it felt. I was emotional, which in women's terms means dramatic.

As the school year began, and my own classes started up, I lost touch with friends. I kept to myself and my cute little apartment with the excuse of homework and papers. To be fair, I had a large amount of that to do. But never too much to exclude people from my world. I felt like that was a better way for me to live, alone and apart, so I didn't trouble anyone with my own torture, my own nightmares. I'm telling you, this depression and darkness thing is the worst! THE. WORST.

One week in September I cried for three days straight. That was a new record for me. School was overwhelming and I wasn't sleeping much. Alexia was mentioned in my emails more often that week, and I just couldn't handle my own life right then. Anyone else ever feel that way? Ever? That your own life is too hard for you at the moment? Man, it is the pits.

My answer to being overwhelmed is to leave town. I know that shocks you. Told you I like to travel. Leaving town is not for the purpose of running away. It is to give me something else to focus on, to remove myself from the situation, so that when I return I have a new perspective, a new outlook on the problem or issue or situation. So I left.

I have a really good friend who is a pilot (I really am blessed and I know it, even if I don't always see it). We flew to New Orleans and spent the weekend walking around Frenchmen Street, eating beignets, shopping at the street vendors, and devouring the best steak I have ever had in my life. (Just typing that is making my mouth water. That's how good it was.)

I got to see a place I had never been before, eat amazing foods, and remember what it felt like to live life without this dark cloud over my head all the time. Prior to leaving, I had prayed for peace. That the peace of Christ would remove this dark cloak covering my eyes, and peace would fill my heart again. On the plane ride back, while staring at the clouds and the green creation that is Louisiana, God gave me the first step on the road to peace. He gave me a corner to turn.

"And now, our God, the great and mighty and awesome God, who keeps his covenant of unfailing love, do not let all the hardships we have suffered seem insignificant to you" (Nehemiah 9:32a NLT). As I returned to "normal" life, this was my prayer. That the suffering I had endured in the last few months would not be seen as insignificant, but as a resource to prepare me for whatever the Lord has for me and my future. I couldn't believe I was praying for that. I couldn't believe I was ok enough to say "thank you for the hurt, now let it be useful." But somehow I was.

Somewhere on the plane, the Holy Spirit had taken my sorrow and made it more of an ache. He had replaced my suffering with a hope for the future. Don't get me wrong, it wasn't instant. I was not all of the sudden happy-go-lucky. Trust me. Healing is a process, depression is a real pit, and climbing out is not easy. But He had given me hope, and hope is a powerful force.

One important thing to note is that this cycle of depression is a nasty beast. There will be good days (stiletto days) and bad days (sweatpants days). Many of which will be back to back or all in the same week, and you will think you have gone to the emotional loony bin. Don't worry, your friends will think so, too. Unfortunately, it is kind of part of the process. You have to work through the ups and downs to find the constant. The new constant. Because the old one isn't there anymore and it won't return. It can't. Life is no longer the same. You just have to realize that's ok and more importantly, that was part of

God's plan for your life. Scary, frustrating, and crazy, but true.

Even now, months later, I still have the bad days. Thankfully they aren't as often, nor as intense as the ones I faced over the first six months of this journey. But they are still there. The important thing to remember is at some point the rollercoaster does stop. You are able to get off and stand on two feet again. It may just take a while to find your balance.

I'm no expert on grief, nor am I some perfect Christian that gets everything right the first time or every time. I do, however, have a strong faith that the Lord will provide for those who are His children. Even on the days where I'm not 100%, without-any-possible-doubt, absolutely sure of that truth, it is true whether I believe that day or not. Because one thing I have learned is feelings are not true. God is true.

7
ENDURANCE

That fall, the days passed quickly, but the nights were long. The weeks and months dragged on but somehow still seemed to end faster than expected. One day I woke up and it was actually November and the weather had finally decided it was fall., which is rare in Texas.

Fall is my favorite season. It has beautiful colors, layered clothing, and cooler temperatures. It also is a glorious display of change and the need for it. I needed that change because somehow I knew that there was more ahead, and it was probably more than I wanted or could realize. The Lord was preparing me for the battle I was fighting within myself. I was praying that He would build me up to be strong. To be a warrior for His namesake. For I knew He had great plans for my life and He was with me, regardless of my emotions trying to tell me I was alone.

I'm a strong person. I've been independently minded since I was 7. Every year on my birthday, my grandpa would ask me how old I was turning. And every year he would say, "Oh 8 is it? Going on 35." I have prided myself in taking initiative, on setting high standards for myself, and achieving great things through hard work. The Lord has given me tremendous opportunities to serve others, to love on people, and to give of my talents in ways I could never dream. So when I look back on these dark months, I now see training. God had chosen this time in my life to train me for the months, years, and experiences ahead. He was preparing me for the work yet to be done. Or the battle field. Or the ministry. Whatever it is He has for me (and I don't know all of it), He has been using this time to build my endurance.

I'm not a runner. I actually hate it. I do it because it is good for me and helps me be able to eat things I want to eat when I want to eat them. Not eating them all the time, but in a healthy balance. Ok to be fair, my running is like half running and half speed-walking. But you get the idea. Running is hard. Running for long periods of time is even harder. People who train for marathons are crazy to me, and I admire them. Because it takes discipline to train for a race months ahead of time. You have to run when you don't want to, for lengths of time that seem impossible, and if you're like me, you sweat. A lot. It's just gross. But in the midst of that pain and sweat, you are building muscle. You are building a better, stronger, more capable body that can endure far better than the body you started with. You are literally challenging your own physical limits. And that is incredibly amazing and encouraging to me.

This year the Lord has made me a runner for His glory. He has conditioned me to survive pain and suffering, to endure what seems like impossible circumstances in order to share His love and faithfulness with others. He has used both rod and staff to guide me in the direction He wants me to go. And man, was it painful. Terrible, really. But all training is, isn't it? At least the training that actually sticks. The lessons you remember best are often the ones you found to be most difficult, are they not?

8
LOST

Before the great invention of the iPhone or GPS, how did we ever get anywhere? I mean seriously. How were we able to find places we had never been before? Roads we didn't know even existed? Locations we'd never seen? We depend on directions all the time, and man, are they easy to get. I tell Siri where I need to go, she pulls up the location options, I choose the right one, and she accesses my Maps app to talk me through how to get there. I mean, how much easier could it get!

Wouldn't it be so nice if God worked that way? Wouldn't it be so much easier if we could tell Him where we want to go, He gives us options to get there, we choose the best one for us, and He verbally talks us through step-by-step how to get there without delay? Goodness, yes!

Somewhere along the depression walk, you start to feel lost. You question why you are there. You ask questions like "Why has God done this to me?" or "What is this for?". One thing I have learned this year is to ask questions. Not in a challenging way, rather in a needing help kind of mentality. Just like consulting a map. You are given options to choose from, decide on a route, plan accordingly and move forward with somewhat confident steps towards the desired location. (Maybe even add in a nice little traffic display? Where the roadblocks are? Right?).

Asking questions is part of the planning, part of the decision making, and part of the healing. I'm not saying doubt the Lord, because He is always faithful, regardless of your feelings. I am saying, however, to ask Him questions because it is how you build trust. Ask Him, who is all-knowing and is the beginning and the end, what is going on. Why is it happening? He will answer you. Maybe not right away or with verbal step-by-step instructions, but there will be an answer.

I found most of the answers to my wandering in Scripture. I found kernels of directions, eternal truths, and heart-wrenching reminders of how loving God is, even if I didn't want to hear it. And yes, I believe there are times when we won't want to hear it. I think there are times we would rather be upset, or sad, or angry, instead of remembering that we serve a God who is loving enough to put you through this, powerful enough to pull you out of it, but also faithful enough to keep you in it for your development of character.

That is what wandering is about, finding character. Finding yourself in Christ. Finding your way to who God is creating you to be. And man is that path full of crazy turns, tight corners, and heavy fog. But with every foggy day, the sun will come and make it disappear. It will break through, break up the particles, and give way to light and clarity. One way or another, it always does.

9
IDOLS

The thing about depression is that it is a tricky business. It is a skewed lens through which you begin to see the world. Everything is dramatically extreme, one way or the other. You see photos of a friend on Facebook and you think "They have the best life ever. It is perfect and always happy. Why don't I have that?" or something bad happens to you and it is suddenly the absolute worst day in the history of days and you don't know how you will ever survive it. Anyone know what I'm talking about here? Sweet. Glad I'm not alone on this one. The thing about depression's fractured view is that is also sets you up nicely to have and form new idols. Let's walk through what I mean by that.

If you are seeing the world incorrectly, and in the midst of depression, it is incorrect, a shift also occurs in what you view as important in life. For instance, you may not have ever had the desire to join a dating website. But suddenly, with this new lens, all you see is everyone else is happy and you want that too, therefore dating someone must be the answer. It must be. Or you are desperate for anyone to understand you. So instead of praying to God and seeking His wisdom and healing, you find solace in a friend or family member. There is nothing wrong with relying on others and seeking guidance, but when you value that more than you value what the Word is saying to you, that person becomes an idol.

Idol worship was something I thought was everyone else's sin. It was nothing I ever struggled with... or so I thought. I didn't bow down to a golden calf or have an abounding love for money. So how could I have an idol?

Idols come in all sorts of sizes, shapes, and colors. Money and gods are just the main ones we tend to focus on when we mention idols. I learned rapidly and painfully, how friends can become idols.

An idol takes up a large amount of your time, talents, and resources in a way that is not honoring God. It is any person or object or thing that replaces God's sovereignty over your life, and stands there in His place. Idols have control over your emotions and your moods, are able to influence your actions, and control your overall well-being. Here's what happened to me. Oh goodness, this one is going to be hard.

When depression struck me hardest, I leaned heavily on a friend that has been in my life now for many years. We don't always agree on everything, but we had survived enough of life together that our differences challenged us to be better. That's some good progress if I do say so myself. But during this depressed state, I began to seek that person's assurance that everything was going to be okay. I would wait to hear from them or not make plans if I thought I could hang out with them. Their responses or approvals had the power to change my mood, mindset, and feelings in the blink of an eye.

They had so much influence over my life, that if I somehow had done something wrong, I would apologize profusely and then think they would hate me now and wouldn't be my friend any longer. It was the catastrophizing depression talking, but you understand what I mean. I gave rule of my life over to someone who both had no idea and who wouldn't "rule" it well even if they did know they had the control.

It was a slow takeover, nothing that happened immediately. I didn't just wake up one morning and think, "Oh you know what, God really isn't doing it for me right now, so I'm going to let this person take over for awhile. They can guide my feelings and tell me everything is okay. They can handle my tears, be my wise counsel. I will spend all my energy and time and resources to make this person happy so that I then, in turn, can be happy too." I didn't just decide to do that. But I definitely ended up there.

I ended up at a place where I was depending on their words or text messages. I was in need of their support and encouragement. But here is the real kicker, I felt like I needed it more than I needed God's support. I longed to have a relationship with this person more than I wanted to have one with God. I put more time and effort into making our friendship better than I did on my making my relationship with the Lord better. And that, my friends, is an idol.

It took me about three months of delusion and spiritual deception to figure out the HUGE blunder I had made, the large sin I had committed. You should have seen me the day I figured all this out. How I cried that day. How could I cast aside the One who loved me, gave His life for me, for a mere, imperfect human? Did I really think that was a better investment? A better use of my time? How did it get this far without me realizing it? I mean, I was reading my Bible and praying to Jesus, and asking for wisdom. How was it that I had an idol in the mix at all?

Here's how: the second we take our focus from knowing the Lord better to just playing the Christian game, Satan is there immediately to feed on our doubts. We look for someone to blame for our sorrows, and think that if even God can't keep this from happening, then obviously He can't help me with the small every day stuff. I just need someone for that. Or so we think and so Satan continues to tell us. What a horrible, sad, and heart-breaking lie.

Once I figured out what had happened, I lost it (not a real surprise, is it?). I didn't just break down and cry, but also begged for forgiveness. I asked the Lord to rid my heart of these stupid, selfish and sinful acts. I prayed that He would take me back to knowing Him and relying on Him only for peace, healing, comfort and support. I asked that He would help me to take my friend off the high honored position I had set them on, and allow them to be only the loving, caring, human friend that they were. No one needs the burden of being someone else's idol. That's a terrible responsibility. I also asked that the Lord would not hold it against them, this sin that I had committed. I know that may sound weird, but I didn't want my sin to blemish the other person.

I say all this to say, be on your guard. Idols are everywhere, in everything, and can very easily become a part of your life when you are not prepared. They are especially keen to show up when you are at your lowest. Since you are already vulnerable and likely not on the closest of terms with God at that point, you seek something to fill the void. Anything that fills that spot is an idol. It can be food for comfort, wine for peace, people for support, working out for healing. Whatever it is, if it stands where God should stand as top priority for your time, talents, resources, mental capacity, and pursuit in life, you have crossed over to the dark side of idols.

None of these things in their proper place in life are bad. It is when they take on a priority role in your life that they become sin. As James says, evil desires turn into sin and sin turns into death. The sin of idol worship is not to be taken lightly, as the first of the Ten Commandments reminds us.

There is forgiveness and healing for the sin of idol worship. It is a difficult process, much like breaking a bad habit. You must go through the hardship, withdrawal, and rebuilding stages of creating new habits. It is painful, time consuming, and often not pretty. But it is needed and worth it. I have never felt closer to my Creator than when I realized He had taken first place in my life again.

10
CHOOSING JOY

Dark, depressing stuff so far. What can I say? It has been a rough year. Even trying to type it into words doesn't do it justice. But the truth is, it doesn't have to. I'm sure you have gone through your own time of sadness, depression, your own hurt. Big or small, hurt is something we all experience. It is part of what makes us human, part of what connects us all. So I know you understand. You get it. You have your own story that is just as painful, maybe even more so. And I want you to know, I am praying for you fervently because depression is real. Sadness and hurt are true things and we have to contend for one another when we are weak. If we don't, who will?

I am here to tell you there is light. I have to confess, I haven't reached a time yet where light is there every day. Some days, maybe. It is getting closer to most days. But it isn't every day yet. I have faith it will be. I don't know when or how, but I know that it will. One day the light will shine again on my days for many days at a time. One day the Lord will restore joy to my heart no matter the circumstances and I will learn to live in joy always just as the Scriptures call us to do.

However, it is a journey. It is a daily reminder that there is and can be hope today and in the days that follow. There is such thing as abounding joy. I have complete confidence that it will be part of my life on a consistent basis without wavering in the midst of life's storms. As Revelation tells us, there is coming a day when there is no more night, no more pain, no more tears. (Revelation 21:4) A day will come when all we will do is stand in the presence of the Lord and praise Him. We will worship at His throne and proclaim His greatness to the masses. How glorious!

Choosing joy is a new concept for me. I have never had to do that before. I have never had to choose joy as a part of my life. It was just always there. But choosing it, having to remind myself to actually pick joy each day, that is completely new to me. Anyone else feel this way? Anyone ever want to just not be happy for a while? Man, misery is a hairy beast. A life-sucking black hole that spirals us out of our own minds and into a world of desperation, panic, and sadness.

Choosing joy is NOT easy. Let me make that well known now. Maybe there are some people that are always calm, cool and collected. They are happy all the time and live in this blissful bubble of joy. If that is you, Lord bless you! Please send me an email and tell me your secret! But the truth is many of us are not happy or joyful all the time. We let circumstances and situations around us define how we feel about ourselves, our lives, our beliefs, and then that is what we display in our actions. We think just deciding to be joyful, will make it so. We forget that it takes work. This is something I am trying desperately to learn, to practice, and then to repeat on a daily basis. Not so that I am happy all the time, because I believe happiness is a fleeting feeling. No, I'm talking about true joy, the unshakeable peace that endures any and every storm regardless of strength, length, or type of situation.

And we, as believers in Christ, have been given the healing balm for all these wounds, all these storms. We have been given the remedy, the elixir of life, the only real

Band-Aid. We have been given Christ. How blessed we are. And how often we forget it.

11
LOVE

It's the middle of the night. I can't sleep. I just spent the better part of the last three hours having a very difficult but honest conversation with one of my favorite people in the whole world. You know, those conversations you don't want to have but have to in order to move on, be better, fix something. Yeah, those. They are awful. But needed every once in awhile. This conversation wasn't a fight or a misunderstanding. It was a love thing. Yeah the L word. Which means it was even more difficult.

From my limited years on this earth, I have learned a few things. One: hard work does pay off and depends on what kind of dividends you are searching for. Two: life is not easy but God is faithful. And three: love is complicated and painful. In both good and bad ways. So I'm wide awake now because I lost love. Yep, this amazing, beautiful, talented, brilliant, graceful (do I need to keep going?) woman lost love in the ultimate, timeless way: being in love with someone more than they are in love with you. Now to the ones that just read that sentence and sighed while nodding in agreement- Bless you. You feel my pain. Those that laughed out loud and smirked, shame on you. You have no heart. Just kidding… maybe.

So here's the short version of the story. My best guy friend in the world is completely opposite of me, literally in every way possible. He likes country and I'd rather listen to pop. He flies planes and drive motorcycles and I sing in musicals and enjoy reading. I could go on, but you get the idea. OPPOSITE. But somewhere along the way of a very bumpy four years, we began to be friends that truly cared about each other despite our differences. And when tragedy struck my life like a backhanded blow to the head, he was the one person that could make me laugh with tears streaming down my face. How can you not fall in a love with a person that makes you laugh instead of cry?

Well, here's the thing, love doesn't always let you choose where or when. No, it just kind of happens. And loving your best friend on accident isn't really something you plan. Nor do you plan to hear they love you but not like that, either. I mean really, who plans to be let down? Disappointed? Defeated? No one. Especially not someone like me who hates to lose. (Goodness, ask my sister. I'm a horrible loser. We can't even play cards without me getting a little testy about losing). So I feel defeated. Upset. Tired from crying (AGAIN!). I'm frustrated that God would let me get so wrapped up in something that wasn't going to happen. Because of course I blame Him for this. He knew my heart. He knew what I wanted, how I was feeling. He knew and He let me go down that path anyway. A path that led me to sadness and tears and feeling like a teenage girl again because a boy didn't like me. It is His fault. Right?

Ok so maybe that last part was a little ridiculous, but you can't say you haven't thought the same thing, especially over another situation that didn't turn out the way you wanted it to. Maybe it was love, a job that wasn't offered to you, a deal that didn't go through, a child who was never conceived, a test that wasn't passed, weight that wasn't lost, family who didn't understand. We have all been there.

Being disappointed is awful. But the real question is: is it God we are disappointed in, or are we mad we didn't get our way? Did we suddenly become the kid in the corner wailing because what we wanted wasn't given to us? What we asked for didn't happen? Sure, we are upset. I think we are allowed to be for a bit. However, after the initial anger, sadness, and frustration melts away, what's left is a raw heart that the Lord can finally speak to because we finally got our agenda out of the way. Ouch. It hurt me to even type that sentence.

But it's true, isn't it? I'm not saying we shouldn't ask for things from God. I think as our loving Father, He wants us to ask Him for anything and everything. But prayer and asking isn't really about us in the first place and we forget that. We forget prayer is really about seeking His will and His guidance and His plans for our lives. Not about us asking for stuff like a child on Santa's lap and hoping it will show up Christmas morning.

So here's what I learned tonight through this lost love thing. One it hurts. Sucks even. Two, when God does not give us what we ask for, He has a reason. And three, I have never been able to feel more like Christ than I do right now. Weird to say at this moment, I know, but let me explain. We are a world of people that rejected Christ. We thought He was crazy. We called Him names, spit on Him, and ridiculed Him. Then we had the smart idea to kill Him and leave Him in the grave. We hated Him. And even still, He loved (loves) us. He gave His life for us. Saved us from eternity in the burning flames of an awful hell. Even though His love went unrequited.

Do you see what I'm saying? I'm saying that in the middle of the night I couldn't sleep because I was so upset someone didn't love me the way that I loved them and then I stopped crying, realizing this must be just a small portion of what the Savior of the world felt on the cross. He loved us to a horrible death and we didn't love Him back, not until much later anyway. Now that is love. Real, eternal, unbreakable, love. And honestly, I'd bet my whole salary (Ok so, I don't make that much. I do work in education, but it is still a living!) He would do it all over again even if it only meant one of us would turn and follow Him. If just one would come to know Him as Healer, Comforter, Beginning and End, Sustainer, Prince of Peace, Almighty, Powerful, Provider, and Friend. He would do it for just one. Wow. Makes my tears and pain seem so very small. Makes my wounded pride seem like nothing but a scratch. And that my friends, is love.

As for me, my heart will heal. Just typing this out has already helped it begin the mending process. Not to take away from the love I have for my friend, that is still there and will most likely remain with me forever. Because we really are that close and I'd rather be friends with him than not have him in my life at all. But it will heal more because of this truth Christ has shown me in my pain: pain is momentary and He is eternal. That in His own suffering He loved us before we even had the chance to love Him back. And He continued to love us, even though it often goes unreturned. What love!

12
PEACE

I was eating dinner with a friend the other day and we were talking about life. We chatted on the good, the bad, the happy, and the ugly. And at the end of a very long year, we both decided this New Year needed to bring peace and joy. It had to, because there were no other options. We could not survive another year like the one we had just had. Or so we believed.

I've already talked about choosing joy a little bit, but peace is closely tied to that. Now when I say peace, I'm not talking about leaning back and letting nothing bother you. I am talking about constancy in the storms of this crazy life, where nothing shakes you. You are able to remain in one piece and with one peace (see what I did there!!) no matter the circumstances. Unshakeable, unbreakable, sustaining calm in the hurricane around you.

So to those of you that have suffered greatly, I can hear what you are thinking, "Ok Rachel, but you don't know what I have been through. You don't understand the pain I have suffered. How is peace even possible?" Peace is possible because we serve a God who does impossible things with ordinary people all the time. In fact, He's famous for it. The Bible in its entirety proclaims His talent for doing insane things no one can fathom and making mundane, regular people into extraordinary heroes for His namesake. Yeah that's right. Heroes. And let me tell you, if He can open the mouth of a donkey and speak truth from that animal to its rider, then He can just as easily bring you peace. (Yes that story is really there. It's awesome and hilarious. Please go read it. It's in the Old Testament. You know, the OTHER part of the Bible…Numbers 32. Go check it out!).

I do not have all the answers. Goodness knows, I am far from the smartest person in the world or even the wisest. Nor am I perfect, though I try to be. It's pride. I'm working on it, ok? Rather, I'm sharing this so that you know you are not alone. We all struggle with this. ALL OF US. Even Miss Perfect in the church pew next to you that somehow managed to get three children into Sunday School on time and put on makeup this morning. Who does she think she is? But even she needs peace from her own storms. And she has them no matter what the makeup says. Or Mr. Works-out-a-lot at the office. (Yeah, you guys thought I wasn't going to hit you too. I'm not that nice.)

Somewhere he found time to out-sell you, perfect his muscles, and stop for Starbucks coffee on the way into the best job in the world. He has demons too. And guess what, one of the biggest protectors from demons is peace. The other is faith. And the third is joy. Peace comes as a gift from the One who calms the storm. We exercise faith in the One that is able, and choose joy in the One that heals all wounds. So it is possible. Because He is Lord of it all anyway.

13
MARRIAGE

Let's just get this out there so you can stop worrying about me. I'm not married. I'm very single. I know you are wondering how such a talented, confident, baseball-loving, cooking, sweet, Christian woman could possibly still be unattached? If I knew that, I wouldn't be writing this chapter. So yeah, that is the big secret. And you know what else, I'm the only one left of my siblings both older and younger that is still single.

Go ahead, I can feel your prayer list for me already being formed in your head. Write it down and mail it to me.

I enjoy mail (I think I've already mentioned this before?). Pray for me all you want. I would covet your prayers, because being single is hard. Just don't send me your sympathy or sadness. Don't send me your pity or your judgment. That you can keep.

Here's the reason why: most days I actually like not being married. Some of you are shocked a woman would even say that out loud. So I'll say it again. Most days I enjoy not being married. How is this even possible you ask? Well for starters, I don't have to share my bathroom with anyone. Especially a boy. They are gross. Yeah I have two brothers, I know it's true. Second, I do what I want. Seriously. Whatever I want to, whenever I want to do it, time and money permitting, I get to do whatever I want to do. If I want to sit and watch episodes of *Arrow* back-to-back all night (have I mentioned yet I love superheroes?), I don't have to consult with anyone to see if the TV is free or if that sounds like fun to them.

Also, I hate football. Yes, I'm from Texas and I don't like football. Basketball and baseball, I'm your girl. But being married during football season just sounds awful. Some of you wives know what I'm talking about, and your season of "trials and tribulations" just so happens to run congruent with the NFL calendar. I get you.

And more important than having to tolerate football, I like being single because my nail polish lasts me a week to 10 days. Really! You moms are doubting me, but think about this. I don't have my hands in dishwater every day, nor am I cleaning up after children, husband, and pets. Yeah it is a nice luxury.

That is most days. Most days I thoroughly enjoy being single. But to be completely honest, there are some days I don't like it at all. Being single is viewed in our society as having some kind of plague you were not lucky enough to get vaccinated from. You laugh, but it is true.

What do you do when someone tells you they are sick? You say, "Oh I'm so sorry! I hope you feel better and are able to get back to normal soon." What do you say when someone says they are single? "Oh I'm so sorry! I hope you don't feel bad and are able to find someone so you can be normal soon." Right? You say that! It has been said to me on countless occasions, or some variation of that. I know you mean well, but come on. Why would you tell me not to feel bad? I don't feel bad. I just told you I have a great life, even taking into consideration hard losses. Something every person has experience with. But really?!? Why would I feel bad? Except for the fact that you just said you felt sorry for me and my entire life somehow went from being awesome to being inadequate in 2.5 seconds flat. Cool. Thanks…

So here is my perspective from a single female that loves the Lord to whoever reads this book: Being single is not a curse or a disease. It is a blessing. So please stop feeling sorry for single people and be supportive of their lives. Give them encouragement as they run a very difficult race called life alone. Yeah that's right. ALONE. You are fortunate enough to have someone with you to share the burden, even if they contribute to the burden sometimes (or maybe all the time).

We are here trying to run the same race as you, with the same hurts and hang ups, in a world that is telling us to be married, to not eat, to work out excessively, to give ourselves over to whatever looks good and is pleasurable and fun for the moment. We are doing all of that by ourselves. Ok? So yeah, don't give us your pity. Instead, give us your encouragement. Encouragement to run the race before us with strength and courage and to have the love and mercies of God at our backs. (And now, I will step off my soapbox).

With that said, I believe marriage is a beautiful thing. I believe it is one of the most holy things on earth. To be bonded with another, under God, for life, no matter what comes. That's HUGE. And the only way that is even remotely possible through two very human people is with the love of Christ at the center of it. I hope one day to experience that kind of love for myself. One day. But that is not in my life right now. Nor am I unhappy with where I am. It is actually possible to live a life that way. And the Lord has used these years to allow me to do some incredible things. Do I wish I had kids of my own? Of course! But currently I play mother to 100+ students and The World's Best Aunt to four nieces. Do I want someone to share my life with? Duh. Who doesn't? But I have been given phenomenal friends and family with which to seek wisdom, comfort and laughter. Is it the exact same? Of course not. Even still I'm not any less happy with this moment in my life than I would be if I were married right now.

14
WAITING

I'm horrible at waiting. Absolutely, horrible. I like plans. I like to see plans executed well. I like to know what is going to happen and when, and then I like to know the exit strategy. There is no time in my life left for waiting. Ever. And I'll be honest, I probably keep my life so busy that waiting would be considered a luxury.

But most of us don't like waiting either, do we? We want a life full of instant potatoes, TV on demand, internet access everywhere, and handheld devices that do everything for us in seconds. We want it simple, easy, and clear-cut. And most importantly, we want everything now. Simply reading the sentence makes me feel like a more selfish individual. I mean, how am I that important of a person that I should demand anything and everything whenever I want it? It is often pleasant to have things conveniently at your disposal. But unfortunately, and fortunately for us, God does not work that way.

No, He's more into doing things in His own time and for His own purposes. Apparently it is called "His will." He's concerned with one thing, and one thing only- bringing a lost world closer to Himself. Of course, there are different byproducts of that endeavor. As members of His family we have access to an invaluable inheritance. It is called eternal life with Him in glory. But we have to wait for that too. I'm telling you, this waiting thing just does NOT go away.

So how do you get good at waiting? How do you practice it without going crazy? How do you let it be part of your life without letting it drown you in silence and unfocused thoughts? You surround yourself with truth. You use the Scriptures and the undeniable evidence of the work God has done in the lives of those around you. You utilize the stories and experiences of courageous people to encourage you during your waiting period. Let their own trials be beacons of hope for yours. Let their lessons be witnesses to coming victories in your own life. Learn to wait well by their examples of God's faithfulness. It doesn't matter if they personally waited well or not. Rather, if you can see God coming through in the end, it will be an encouragement to you, right?

These people that you surround yourself with, that serve as examples are called mentors. They are wiser individuals who have lived through more life experiences than you. They don't have to look like you or sound like you or even have the same dreams in life as you, but they do have to be willing to share their lives with you. They have to want to help you as much as possible by sharing their experiences, coaching you on decisions, and offering advice when it is most needed.

These people should be strong, Christian ambassadors. Leaders of the faith and doers of the Word. They are the ones who have the love of Christ radiating from their faces. All He has done for them and through them in their journey will shine. They don't have to be older, though they often are. They don't have to be rich and successful, but they are likely very blessed in many areas of life. They won't have a perfect life (no one does!), though you may think they do by looking at them.

These mentors are people who will contend in prayer on your behalf before the throne of God. They will pull you out of the depression pit you are sinking in and get you back to the glorious presence of Christ. They have been there and know victory is possible and just around the corner.

Find mentors. Very soon I will be writing a whole dissertation on the effects of mentoring on college student success, but until that happens just take my word for it. Mentors are important and impactful. I have three of them.

One acts as a spiritual mentor. She is who I go to when I have God questions. For example, why is He doing this? Where does the Bible say this? How does this all really end in Revelation? That kind of thing.

Then there is one that acts as a life mentor, offering advice and clarity on situations. He is my go-to person when life is overwhelming. He is my biggest supporter and advocate outside of my family. He is always on my team. Everyone needs a person like this. Everyone.

The third is a career mentor, someone who is where I would one day like to be in my career. So she coaches me on paths that I can take to get there and encourages me to keep going.

These people have changed my life. Having mentors in your life will change yours.

15
OUTLETS

Obviously, I've learned a few things about myself this year. I've learned about the best sides of me and the dark, never-want-to-leave-my-bed sides of me. I've learned to keep moving forward (even if it is centimeters instead of miles that day) regardless of how I feel, because sometimes that is the best thing for you. Whether you believe it is relevant at the moment or not.

Outside of prayer and crying (it can be therapeutic!), I learned what my outlets are. You know, the things you do that take your mind off anything no matter how bad. The release you need to refocus and gain perspective. Those are your outlets. Here is what I've learned about my own outlets.

Outlets are hobbies on steroids. They are the opportunity to escape your current world, quiet your mind, and renew your spirit. Many people have creative outlets. They write music, paint, draw, take photos, etc. I have a few things I do depending on the level of escape that is needed. Before I divulge my remedies, please understand prayer is a key factor in overcoming my stress. But the following things often help me gain perspective by providing a measure of distance while in prayer, or give me the chance to pray more clearly and without anger.

Level 1. If is has been a stressful day for any reason and I am simply tired, I come home and cook dinner. I really enjoy deciding on a meal and then going about getting lost in making something delicious to eat. Sometimes I pair that with a glass of red wine. Then I put on a TV show or movie or read a book and let the day melt away. This is the easiest outlet for me, and is applied to the most basic level of stress requiring a remedy (i.e. a long day, a stressful email, a simple word spoken to me that was careless).

Level 2. If the day was really bad, physical activity is not only needed, but essential so I can function in front of people the next day. There were many days this past year where I couldn't sleep and went to the gym as a way to do something besides tossing and turning. There were also days when I went to the gym because if I didn't strain every muscle in my body I was going to punch someone in the face. Clearly not very Christian of me, but true. I'm just being honest. I don't have Christian thoughts 100% of the time. Let me know when you find someone that does.

Level 3. This is the emotional day where somehow at the end of every sentence I end up crying. Man, those are rough! This type of day requires me to draw or paint or craft something in general. I literally have to create something beautiful in order to justify the day and compensate for the ugliness that was flung upon me that day. I'm sure you can guess I had a lot of DIY projects this past year... a lot.

Level 4. After multiple days of exhaustion, frustration, stress, or sadness, I have to get out. I literally have to leave town. I mentioned this before, but it is unreal how much better I feel after I remove myself from the situation and how refreshed I am when I return. Regardless of whether situations actually improved or not, I at least return with a better perspective than when I left, and can more clearly see what is going on. This is the highest level of release for me, getting away. Gratefully it isn't needed all the time, even through this last year held more times where the only outlet that would help anything was to get out of town.

That's it. Four levels. Each with a different outlet related to the release that is needed. Yep that's right. Four different levels. Go ahead and judge me, either as too complicated, or just plain crazy. But perhaps you aren't so different.

You have levels of stress and outlets you've created to handle the stress. You either consciously or subconsciously have some method that facilitates your return to a normal state. We are built this way. We have been built and armored to withstand trials and beatings. The Lord has equipped us to grow in wisdom and stature. One way we can do that is by listening to His voice. I strongly believe the Lord will use our outlets to speak to us. Because they often are able to quiet our minds. These escapes serve as a microphone through which we can hear the voice of the Lord more clearly. Because when things have been crazy and we have actually stopped thrashing and are finally quiet, maybe even broken in heart, then we can know and understand what the Lord has been trying to tell us all this time. He uses our outlets to reveal Himself to us.

16
LOSING IT

This past year, while being one of the saddest, was also one of the most victorious. This year, above many of the other years I would call "successful" was by far one of the most rewarding. I know what you are thinking. I just spent half of a book explaining all the terrible, depressing things that this past year brought with it. And that is all true and very real. The personally rewarding part in particular, came at the beginning of the year. I now have come to refer to them as the ignorant months. Ignorant, in that I had no idea what lay ahead for me, and I was pretty happy living in my blind bliss.

My victory? I lost it. Completely lost it. All 40 pounds of it. That's right. I kicked my butt into high gear and decided it was time to be who I was and look how I felt. It was time to work hard, sweat like crazy, and look awesome. And guess what? I did it. Yes, I was gorgeous before (inside and out, and oh, so humble…) but something wasn't right when I looked in the mirror. I saw someone I knew but didn't feel connected to anymore. I was tired of feeling that way. So it was time to change that.

I woke up December 27, 2013 and decided that was the day my life would change. I didn't wait until New Year's Eve to make a resolution. I didn't do hundreds of hours of research to decide the best approach. I simply made the decision to change my life and I did. Over those six months, and even to this day, people ask me what I did to lose 5 pant sizes in 6 months' time. I tell them what I am going to tell you now how to completely lose it.

First, that December morning I woke up and decided to change my life was a decision I came to on my own. No one else was suggesting I do it. No one was even doing it with me. It was my choice and it was just me. By myself. That's where the drive comes from. It has to be your decision. No one else can make it for you, or force you to do it, or bully you into it. It has to be you.

Second, I enlisted accountability in a couple of forms. One being technological. I bought a FitBit (I have the Zip model if you really want the specifics) and downloaded the My Fitness Pal app to my phone. I was going to count everything I did, energy in and energy out. I was going to know what sources of fuel where being put in my body and what I was doing to use that fuel up in great ways.

I never went on a 'diet'. EVER. Here's why: they don't last. Real life catches up to you and you finally realize you can't NOT eat cheese or bread or cake ever again. That's dumb. I decided that I would adjust my food choices with some substitutes (like Greek yogurt for regular yogurt because it has more protein), and learn to balance out what I wanted to eat (such as cheesy carbs like pizza, pasta, nachos) with what my body needed. I figured out that if I wanted a burger for dinner (and I do eat turkey, black bean, and quinoa burgers along with beef ones) then I was going to have to have a salad for lunch to balance out calories. Then additionally, most likely, I would have to spend an extra 10-15 minutes on the treadmill if there was cheese on the burger. I also drank a lot of water, but I feel like that should be a given.

So I played this game of recording everything I put in my body on that app. It was insane but I kept with it. And I let my FitBit take care of how much I moved and man, did I move! I used any excuse to get in my 'steps' for the day. I would park at the last spot in the parking lot to take 10 extra steps. When a commercial came on, I would walk circles around my apartment. At my office, I would walk the whole floor before I went to the restroom and the whole floor on my way back from it. Not only is the mental break nice, but the movement refocused my brain and I was getting in more steps.

Another rule I made for myself was to watch any TV only on a treadmill. Basically, I had to be moving to watch something by myself. And it worked. My goal was to do 10,000 steps 3- 4 times a week. To reach that, I usually had to work out 3 or 4 times a week or include walking at the mall or grocery store, playing at the park with my nieces, or walking around campus for meetings for one day's goal. Either way, I used any opportunity to move and keep myself moving. My friends thought it was funny how religious I was about it, right up until they started noticing the difference. Then they were asking me what I was doing different, and this was my answer: I was choosing to move more. I was choosing to be an active participant in the big, beautiful life around me rather than be one that literally sat and watched it happen.

The other form of accountability I enlisted was human. I told everyone my goal. My family, my friends, anyone that would listen. I wanted them all to know that I was changing my life and I expected them to help me keep this promise to myself. I didn't want them to get mad at me when I didn't finish a meal or get upset at me if I told them I had to work out and not go out to eat. I wanted them to be on my team, checking in on my progress, and encouraging me to keep going regardless of the results. I used them as fuel to motivate me to keep at it and as validation that I was doing the right thing.

The last form of accountability I desperately needed was spiritual. I know some of you are thinking, "How is that even possible?" Here's what I mean. I prayed fervently that the Lord would give me the strength and confidence in myself to accomplish this goal, to work hard, to see results, and to be a good steward of the body He has given me. That's right I prayed for weight loss. You may call it crazy or magical thinking all you want, but the Lord will give you desires and then help you accomplish it. And my heart was needing a body that showed someone who was capable of handling anything in front of her and was a vessel the Lord could use for any and everything. How could He send me if I wasn't prepared? I had read His word, I knew songs about Him, but my body was physically not ready to do His work.

And the only way for me to have any chance of that happening were to enlist His help. To seek His guidance and strength and power to be able to put one foot in front of the other and keep moving forward.

I credit my success with weight loss to finding real balance in what I want and what I need. And then even more so, I credit it to the God who makes seemingly impossible things possible. And He did that for me in a very tangible way. He took me out of myself and placed me on a rock that was surer than sure and gave me the ability to see this goal through. And I did just that. With the help of lots of prayer, many people's encouragement and many, MANY hours of sweat I was able to accomplish this daunting goal.

Also as a side note when losing weight, find something other than food to reward yourself with when you reach your goals. For me it was nail polish (I know, super girly!). But I like expensive nail polish, so it was a treat to me to get a new color for every 5 pounds that I lost. And it made me feel good to reward myself with something that wasn't counterproductive to my goal of losing weight. So I encourage you to find a reward that will be celebratory of your achievement and not be counter to the things are you are trying to implement and change in your lifestyle.

From there, the pounds started to come off. Slowly but surely they began to drop off of my body. It took me a while to even notice a difference and took family and friends even longer. But once they did, it felt like every day someone was asking if I had lost weight, or telling me I was looking great. That is one of the BEST feelings in the world. Again, this was not a "I lost 20 pounds overnight and now my life is perfect" kind of thing. Goodness, no. My story is I ate carrots when I wanted chips because pizza was on the menu for dinner and I had to balance it out. I went to the gym so that I could eat what I wanted and still stick with my plan. It is a story of hard work, practical food selections, and perseverance during the times I didn't think it was actually working. Because after all the weight was off came the fun part: SHOPPING!

Another thing to note here is this all occurred in the first half of the year. I finished my goal before I felt like the bottom of my life dropped out from under me. I think that was on purpose. The Lord knew what was coming. Retrospectively, He was preparing my body to know its limits, to have outlets for releasing energy, and to not seek food as my comfort in the days ahead.

Even through deep depression, I was able to maintain my weight loss and stay healthy. If I had not done this the first half of the year, I cannot honestly tell you what size I would be today. I can't know I would be able to handle this amount of loss and not instantly gain 20 pounds. In fact, that could have been very possible. But the Lord knew what I needed to do and when I needed to do it. And He helped me to complete this goal and prepare for the days of loss ahead without my even realizing it at the time. He knew. He equipped me. He is faithful.

17
ART OF BUSYNESS

You know those people that can do everything? That super mom? Or the insane coworker that outdoes everyone, raises family of four, and coaches all of their Little League teams? Yeah, you know. Those people. Don't hate me, but I'm one of them. I am always busy. And for the most part, I enjoy my life that way. When I have nothing to do I am bored and wondering if I'm missing something. I do my best to always have something going on, whether it is people to see, projects to work on, places to go, or lives to change. Just to give you an idea, here is what my day looked like today.

I woke up at 7 AM because I'm still working on being a morning person. I got ready and dressed, and then went to the grocery store before work. Being busy, that was the only time I could go and get food so I would make it through the week with something in my kitchen. I came back to drop off groceries, and then headed into work around 9 AM. At which point I sifted through the 50+ emails that had magically appeared in my inbox overnight, I then headed out to one of the five meetings on my calendar for the day.

The hours between 10 AM and 12 PM are kind of a blur, but I think I got some work done…? I had a lunch training session to lead, a student leadership meeting to attend and a class to teach. I finally left campus at 6 PM, which is early for me on a Wednesday, to begin my own stack of homework. Classes started yesterday for the second semester of my doctoral program. I am a full-time graduate student and a full-time employee at the university. That translates to 40+ hours of work each week, and three doctoral classes to manage and excel in.

One of those three classes is statistics. Math and I do NOT get along. Since birth, it has been a constant battle between me and numbers. Somehow I have survived them, but just barely and typically after many tearful battles with the textbook and calculator. I've just spent four hours trying to reteach myself a subject I forgot immediately after my final during my master's statistics course over four years ago.

Now I am sitting in my apartment writing about being busy because it is all I can think about at the moment. I should be sleeping and all I can think is, "How did I get this busy?" and "How in the world am I going to survive it?"

That, is a VERY normal day for me. And I didn't even mention the stress that came with reading and answering some of the emails that were in my inbox today. I have a lot going on and it is just me! I don't have to factor in spouses, kids, or pets. Just me and my crazy schedule. But the truth is, we all have crazy schedules. We all have jobs, classes, families, friends, hobbies, health, etc. We have things that occupy our time, talents, resources, minds, and spirits. And at the end of it all, we are busy and tired individuals that simply need rest.

I'm awful at resting. I was the child in our family that hated taking naps. I would always get caught making noise or singing during naptime. In fact there is a horrifically embarrassing story my dad tells about me messing around at naptime that somehow always gets brought up at family functions. You can ask him about it when you see him. I'm sure he will tell you. To this day if I am able to "rest" during the day, it is a 20 minute power nap unless I am sick or exhausted from crying too much.

Even if I am supposed to sit and watch a movie, I somehow end up looking at Pinterest, cooking dinner, doing laundry, or writing chapters in this book. I am never still. I literally have to remove myself completely from my normal surroundings, turn off my phone and email, and not have anything scheduled to do but read a book for a week before rest even feels like it is a part of my life. I have a problem, and I am working on it.

This art of busyness is a blessing and a curse. Blessing in that I am able to do many things and get many more things done. I am proud of my motivation to always be moving and working on something, and thankful for my ability to multitask. But man, can it be stressful! I can look at all the mess that was a day like today and have complete faith that I will survive it, though I have no idea how.

But the truth is, many times busyness is there to keep us distracted from what is actually important. We can argue many of the things on our daily list are important, but I have to sit and wonder, "Are they really?" Family, yes definitely important. Doing your job that pays bills, important. Completing assignments for school, important, if you want a diploma. So there are good things we do that add value to our lives and should be placed in a higher position than others. But at the end of your day/month/year/life, the only busyness that really matters is the activity of knowing Christ, loving Him, developing your relationship with Him, and seeking His wisdom and truth. And isn't that exactly the first thing to get taken off the list when life gets too cramped?

Some of you read that question and an ache formed in your heart because you know that is where you are. Others nod your head in agreement because you have been there. We will all be at one of those two places in life at some point. We will all experience crazy schedules, insane hours, overloaded to-do lists, and demanding deadlines. But the only way we will be victorious over them is if we place our priorities with the One who is in all things, of all things, and rules over all things.

So easily I forget I am not in this busy battle alone. But the Lord is contending for my heart to stop, be still and rest in Him because He is taking care of everything else, even statistics! He will show His power and love and unfailing mercies, and will sustain me while still giving me the strength to keep moving forward. How cool is that?

Rest for me requires a few things. First of all, I literally have to leave town for more than a week. Four days is not enough, as I am just getting to the point where I am comfortable doing nothing by the end of day three. To return directly after making it to that point means no restful nights. So I need a whole week off of work and out of town by myself or with one to two other people. Out of the country is usually the best, but with my educator's paycheck, it doesn't happen very often.

So a whole week out of town, email turned off on my phone, my phone left in the hotel room, or I give myself a rule to only look at it for a certain amount of time each day and that is it. Then I have to have no schedule and set no alarms. I wake up when I wake up, I go where I want to go, see what I want to see, eat when and where I want to eat, and generally have no set plans for the entire week. I read books, watch movies, lay on the beach, get lost in museums, drink tea, and take my time with every meal. I have meaningful conversations with someone on the trip with me, unless I'm alone and then I journal. At this point, my mind is finally quiet. My heart isn't racing at slightly higher levels and my soul is at rest. That is what it takes. Sad, isn't it? Again, I'm still working on it.

But something I am trying to understand more is to rest in Jesus every day. He commands us to do so, and here I am saying it takes me seven whole days to feel normal again. That's dumb. I look at the semester I have ahead of me, the work, the assignments, the challenges known and unknown, and have complete confidence I will be able to survive this. But the real question is, will I be able to rest through it? Will I find the way to rest in Christ and be a good steward of my resources to get done what needs to be done?

The truth is, I know this will only happen IF I rest in the Lord. It will only be successful IF I lean on His strength and not my own. I will only remain standing IF I lay my selfishness down and don't think I can do this all on my own. Because I can't. There is literally no human way it is possible for me to do it alone. So I must learn to rest and that begins with starting my day in the right mindset and with the right priorities.

This year I have decided to study the concept of joy. So each morning I read verses containing joy and a theological concept of joy that we as Christians are called to apply. I use this time to realign myself with what is really important: Jesus, joy and prayer. Everything else will take care of itself. And you know what? It actually helps me face the day ahead. It helps me remember I am not in this by myself, but He is with me and will be with me throughout this day. Do I have it perfect? Goodness, no. If I did, I would give you a step-by-step program to living a busy-free life that still leaves you feeling productive and full. No. I don't know exactly how that works, but I do know it starts with prayer and daily "quiet/ restful" time with Christ.

Another book I read while on a plane to a conference was called "Crazy Busy" by Kevin DeYoung. I loved this book for a few reasons. One, it was short. And any book on busyness should be short, because ain't nobody got time to read a long book on busyness. Duh. Two, it related being busy to biblical principles. Is being busy really biblical or are we messing things up? Third, it hit home. One point in particular.

In one of his final chapters, DeYoung defined busyness as you thinking that you are the only person that can do that job, whatever it is, and everyone else will get it wrong. You are putting yourself and your skill set above everyone else. Making your work and your thought processes superior to everyone else. This is my own summary, not DeYoung's words. Go check out his book for yourself to see what you may gain from his wisdom.

I finished that chapter and closed my eyes, asking God if that was what I was doing? Was I going into work thinking I was the only one who could do that project correctly? Or get the assignment done before anyone else? Did I really think I was that irreplaceable?

The answer, unfortunately, was a resounding yes. I did think I was the linchpin of all operations. I thought I had to handle everything because no one else could. This is obviously not true and I am not THAT valuable. I work hard and love what I do. I'm actually pretty good at it. But that doesn't mean others aren't able to take responsibility for other parts of the program, other areas and projects that need to be done. I started to realize the only way for me to be less busy was to allow others to take ownership and participate alongside me.

I wish I could tell you I have mastered this, but I haven't. I'm still working on it. I had a conversation with my boss about it and he is helping me delegate tasks and projects so that I am working normal hours and not taking on too much responsibility all the time. So my encouragement to you if busyness is really a problem for you, is to recruit help. Have someone in your office that will call you out, take things off your plate, and remind you to let someone else handle it. Not because you aren't capable, but because you have plenty of other equally important things to be working on.

18
THAT ONE THING

We all have one. You know, that thing. That one thing that sits in your mind and heart and has the ability to cripple you at any given moment. That one fear or desire or want or need or doubt. It's constantly there reminding you of who you aren't instead of who you are and Whose you are. It can be horrifying or terrorizing depending on the day. Some days it sits quietly and you almost forget that it still has a prominent place in your innermost being. Now before you go on to tell me you are too good for that, I'm going to tell you about my own "one thing."

Ready? Ok, here it goes. I have a fear of being forgotten. That at the end of my life no one will remember me, have good things to say about me, want to attend my funeral, or even know I was gone. That is my biggest fear. I fear being so insignificant in this life, to this world, and to the people around me, that I will leave it without anyone noticing.

I have this deeply entrenched, soulful ache that I could leave this world unchanged and unmarked by my own existence. It's a terribly, heart-wrenching feeling. And it attacks me at the most inopportune times. And just latches on, sucking life and love and joy from my life. Minute by minute, tear by tear. Slowly it replaces all of my happiness in the Lord with a burdening, dark cloud of loneliness, unworthiness, and dreadful doubt.

I can't say for sure where this fear came from. I am and have always been supported in my family to follow my dreams and do amazing things. To be the best that I can be and live as an example of Christ. I was fairly good at many things in life, not great mind you, but good. Think good at lots of things but not fantastic at any one thing in particular. Jack of all trades in an average, mediocre way. I was never chosen last for a team nor was I chosen first. I had many wonderful friends growing up, several still part of my life even decades later.

So I'm not quite sure how this seed was planted, but I do know it is a very real struggle that this independent, driven woman wrestles with all the time. When you are depressed you already think no one cares about you or is concerned about your wellbeing. You live in this world of lies that get disguised as truths. The lies being that you are alone and no one understands or wants you. That you have nothing of value or nothing to contribute to those around you. Unchecked, these lies entice you to withdraw because you believe it is better for everyone else if you do. You see it as self-sacrificing and a worthy act for the greater good of others. That's all a complete and utter lie. Here's the truth.

Not one of us is insignificant or unworthy or unloved. We are all precious daughters and sons of the Most High. We are cherished and valued, fought for and redeemed. We are valiant and courageous. Sure-footed and strong. We have the ability to encompass peace and joy, love and kindness, self-control and gentleness, patience and goodness. And they are in us, because He is in us. I can't tell you how long it took me to understand that THIS was the truth and not the other whispers in my ear the devil was planting. I still have days where I hear those lies, feel their grip in my soul, and have to stop and remind myself Who I really belong to.

It can sometimes be a daily battle that I fight. Most recently it has been more of a random attack, so it throws me off guard more than I'd like. You would think I'd expect it by now, but when life is finally going well and the sun is actually shining and I'm rocking my stilettos, the last thing I am thinking about is being beat down. And yet, here I am on a Thursday night beat down because I was sideswiped by the crafty one himself. How does that keep happening when I least expect it? How do I stop him from taking over my mind with unbearable things that threaten to steal my joy and my peace of mind?

Here's how, I beat the devil by equipping myself for the battle. Daily. By reading the Word every morning to know what it says, and allow it to remind me that I'm not alone. That there are stronger beings at work on my behalf. Then I fight back by surrounding myself with people that know my demons and will call them out to me lovingly, or not, depending on what I need that day. By filling your home, your desk, your phone, with reminders of those that love you, words of encouragement, and prayers for those around you. Nothing helps you rid yourself of your demons more than praying for that deliverance for others.

This week alone, I have greatly struggled with being forgotten. It is a reasonable fear to have as a single person. It is that old fear of dying-alone-with-no-one-to-realize-it kind of thing. But really, I just want to make sure I am remembered. I don't have to change the whole world, but I want to change someone's world. I don't have to negotiate world peace, but maybe offer inner peace to someone around me. I know I can't prevent world hunger, but I can feed the souls of the students who enter my office on a daily basis. I may be alone as far as martial status goes, but that does not keep me from expressing love to others. Even if it isn't the one person I want to show me love back, or to remember my name, or to understand my need for quality time, or to know my God, or to see my pain and success both as beautiful blessings from the Lord. Even then, I cannot let the lies take hold of me. I am already rescued from it. Already redeemed and guarded in the blood of Christ.

Even Paul had that one thing nagging him. That thorn in the flesh. That ache that stole his breath in the middle of the night, that caused him pain and suffering and tears. So if we are counted with him in history, maybe we can see this pain, these lies as our thorns. Maybe we can see this wound as a mark of holiness instead of a deficit of attributes?

What is your one thing? What causes you distress and horrifying pain you are barely able to stand? I pray that you will find the strength to clothe yourself for the battle ahead. That you will realize you are not alone. That you will know there are many fighting with you, beside you, and ahead of you. That our great Lord is the victor, always.

19
BEGIN AGAIN

This has been a developmental year in my life. I hope every year is developmental, but this last one included pivotal changes in the direction of my life. Maybe it was just time for the Lord to reveal Himself to me in new and extreme ways. Maybe it was just time for me to change and it took a large amount of pain and struggle to bring about that change. Whatever the reason, the Lord was at work and continues to be in my life on a daily, often hourly, basis.

The other amazing thing is He has given me a new year, a new day, and a new opportunity to experience His love for me and share it with others. He has given me good news of great joy in some very dark days in addition to equipping me for whatever may lie ahead. Funny thing is, I think the hardest, most difficult days are yet to come. Some of you may say that that sounds pessimistic, but others see it as a wise observation. Here's why I believe it is wise.

We as Christians are guaranteed trials and tribulations, struggles and suffering. It is part of the path to being made more like Christ and it is a part of this journey we take in fellowship with others as believers. The Lord did not say that you would be successful or that this world would be easy or even simple. He actually said it would be difficult, trying, and painful in nature. And yet even then, He has promised to be with us. He has given His spirit to lead us and comfort us through whatever obstacles are ahead. That is why I say there are more difficult days ahead.

Here's one way to think about it. When you are learning to lift weights, something I'm still working on, you are building muscle. You start with lighter weights and do a small amount of reps. As you increase in strength, you increase the weights and the number of reps. You add more on. That is the same thing the Lord does when training up His champions. He starts by allowing small weights to come into your life and slowly adds more. He adds demands, trials, overwhelming circumstances, dark days (weights) and He increases the frequency or reps. He is building us up to be A) more like Him and B) strong contenders for the faith.

I am not saying He gives us difficult times just because He can. Rather, He gives us difficult times to develop our endurance as James 1 says, and to cause us to lean into Him. As independent beings, we have the tendency to think we have life handled, and when life is going well we think this theory is correct. It isn't until the storm hits, the world goes topsy-turvy, or the bottom falls out, that we actually stop to acknowledge we can't do this alone and we need Him more than we realize. We have to lean in closer to Him to even begin to consider if we can survive. We need Him. All the time. Every moment of every day. And sometimes we need very large, life-shattering events to kick us off our high, independent, self-reliant horses in order to realize it.

So I get a new chapter. You get a new chapter. We are given the opportunity to grow, change, develop, and most importantly, to learn our desperate need for a Father who loves us unconditionally. He graciously gives us another chance to be His light to an ever-dimming world. Even though we could fail, He allows us another try so that we will draw closer to Him. And this new beginning is yours for the taking everyday, because His mercies are new with each sunrise. You must choose to take it!

This new beginning is something I have prayed fervently for. Though it was always mine to have, the hurt was fresh and so consuming, I honestly couldn't believe I was able to be made new at the start of a new day. Part of me didn't want to be made new. I wanted to sit and cry, feel the sorrow deep in my bones, be angry, throw things, and sulk. Straight up throw a little kid tantrum in the middle of a rainstorm and yell at the sky. Ok, maybe that's a bit much, but something like that. I was hurt, upset, and thought my anger was the only thing keeping me sane. I was choosing not to take the fresh start the Lord was offering me. I didn't want it. But boy, did I need it.

I remember praying over the last year, "Lord, please just take this away. Give me something else to deal with or handle, but take away the pain, heal my heart, and snuff out my anger. Because it is a hot consuming fire taking over my soul right now." Literally those thoughts and words poured from my pen as I prayed (I write down my prayers just as a side note. I'm sure you are shocked to hear that... Not.). I was holding tightly to my anger while still praying for peace, the return of joy, the renewing of my spirit, and a new beginning. I didn't get what I was asking for not because the Lord wasn't giving it to me, but because I was standing in the way of His work.

Is that ever you? You ask for things from the Lord, but your bitterness, anger, or hardened heart is the reason you don't hear from Him? Or you don't think you hear from Him?

The truth is He is answering, you just aren't listening. I was there. I wasn't listening and for a while I didn't even WANT to listen. That's how far I had gone from the Lord at the time. I still talked to Him because I knew I should but I didn't want His answers even though I knew it was what I needed most. I am a selfish, stubborn child who needed to be taught a lesson. And the Lord knew just how I would listen, through more trials, more breaking down, and more pressure.

I have never been more thankful to see a new year in my entire life. To be given the opportunity to start over with a new perspective, new knowledge, and a renewed spirit. What a joy to be able to sit here and type that sentence to you. I'm not naïve enough to think it is puppies and sunshine from here on out. I know there will be many trying days ahead. But I am joyful to say, I am now better equipped for those days than I may have ever been.

When will you allow your new chapter to begin? When will you release your anger or hardships with open hands so that healing can finally take root? When will you decide there is so much more out there for you than sulking in your brokenness? I pray today is your day of renewal. Your day of courage to let go of a hurtful past and take hold of your hopeful future. I pray today is your Day One of a new and exciting way of life the Lord is providing for you. That from now on, you will have the strength to put on your stilettos and begin again.

CLOSING

This process of writing my story has been very cathartic for me over the last few months. It has been an encouragement to see family and friends' feedback as I have worked on this project, and their never-ending love and support as they read the words of my life. They knew some of my experiences before reading my manuscript, but many were so hidden away that there were times I didn't realize their existence, let alone be able to speak them out loud.

I wrote this book for me. I wanted to put a physical form to the amazing things I have seen and learned this past year. When I started, I had no intention of sharing this with anyone outside of my family and close friends. But I have been reminded that the Lord works through us in unique and beautiful ways, and that maybe someone else would benefit from my story. Another heart would be encouraged from knowing at least one other person out there feels the same way they do. I pray that is true. I pray that you have been encouraged, challenged, and strengthened by reading these words. Not by my words, but by the lessons the Lord has been using to refine in my life and invoke great change.

As I tell many of my students, you were created for great and mighty things. It is high time you started acting like it. I say this to them through the lens of love, just as I say it to you now. We were created for more than an average life. But rather, for a life full of amazing and extraordinary things. The only way we prepare for this kind of life is to go through the training for such aspirations, to allow the Lord to work in mighty ways that bring about change for our benefit. I pray you are open to His plans for your life, the sweatpants days along with the ones made for breaking out the stilettos. Both are His gift to you and your future.

One last thing to leave with you. Back in high school, I found this verse to be encouraging and ever since, it has served as my life verse. Each year it means something different to me. This year it means there is a light with joy at the end of whatever dark tunnel I am currently in.

So don't get tired of doing what is good. Don't get discouraged and give up. For you will reap a harvest of blessing at the appropriate time. - Galatians 6:9 NLT

All my best,

Rachel

SIGHTS & SOUNDS

I found out pretty quickly in grad school how I write papers to the best of my ability. Writing this book turned out to be no different. My process includes listening to good music, watching a movie I have seen so many times I could quote it, or simply giving into those middle of the night inspiration sessions that wake me from my sleep.

But in case you want to know what helped me fill the silence while I was typing, I've listed my writing playlist, so to speak. I'm so very thankful for artists who can create something new. One of these days maybe I'll have the time and expertise to create my own music. Until then, I will let these artists do what they do best!

Music

Taylor Swift

Lauren Daigle

Maroon 5

The Fray

Lincoln Brewster

Elevation Worship

OneRepublic

Mat Kearney

The Script

Hunter Hayes

Cody Fry

Film

Star Trek

Skyfall

Valentine's Day

Harry Potter

Pride & Prejudice

Hunger Games

ABOUT THE AUTHOR

Rachel is a lover of Jesus, education, music, DIY projects and travel. She spends her days helping college students realize their dreams, and her nights realizing her own as she studies for her doctorate in higher education. She lives in Dallas with family close by and is the honored aunt of four beautiful nieces.

Made in the USA
Charleston, SC
07 May 2015